Resurrection of Pain

Resurrection of Pain

My Eulogy of Myself

Sailendra Nath Datta

PARTRIDGE
A Penguin Company

Partridge books may be ordered through booksellers or by contacting:

Partridge India
Penguin Books India Pvt.Ltd
11, Community Centre, Panchsheel Park, New Delhi 110017
India
www.partridgepublishing.com
Phone: 000.800.10062.62

To

Panditmashai, P.K.C. and B.K.C.,
the departed teachers of Sanskrit
and English, in the formative years
of school and college life, who had
immensely contributed towards my
development of self and character.

Contents

Preface

Most poems are monologues of the poet. Or, some may be labeled as dialogues between his two selves, the speaker and the listener, the apparent and the inner. And thus the poem becomes his statements, queries, his prayers, tributes, his protests, revolt, his quest, dreams, and his wishes and so on. Those may be simple or complex, depending upon the topic and treatment.

As for myself in the following poems, written over a period of last two years or so, there are glimpses of personal reflection, national issues or human problems, still present and prevalent. Whatever they may be, I've dealt them in a straightforward way; that means, not so 'poetically'. Thus, many of my poems may appear to be rather 'un-poetic' or prosaic, or no better than ordinary rhymes. That, to be excused, is my exact weakness or strength. So far as my content is concerned, I'm rather confident and comfortable in this form, and hence such treatment!

Stylistically, again, I think the selected poems below may appear like prose, rather than poetry. The language may be as simple as possible, but there is very little 'poetic embellishment', as readers of poetry are wont to expect and enjoy. What happened, actually, with me is that I did not overcome the vortex in my mind during the development of an idea or philosophy in each of these poems—I've rather let myself be floated adrift on the tide of the moment. The overflow of feelings—hidden or expressed—has been spontaneous in the sense that they evoked a reaction, a random or definite response in that whirlpool. I've been, it seems, swept in the temporal direction. My spiritual self, although, protects me from a shallow immersion!

September 11, 2013
Kolkata

1. Fortune Arrives At a Slow Pace

Fortune arrives at a slow pace—
So the unfortunate people like to say.
Besides, fortune is quite very fickle—
She likes no place for ever to stay.

Luck upon luck, little by little,
Fortune bestows her good favour
Upon the brave and adventurous few
Who are indeed intelligent and clever.

You can achieve success by efforts only—
May it be dear money or sweet freedom!
Only a sleeping wish wouldn't be enough,
Even tiny ants work hard in act-dot-com.

When the lion gets old and can seldom hunt,
He has to go hungry quite off and on.—
So be up and doing, that's your given lot;
Let fortune smile only when you carry on.

2. Love Has a Rhyme and Reason

Love doesn't break relationship—
It always builds it up for you and me.
Love your neighbours as you would love
Your near dear ones in the family.

Love attracts love and thus
You can create a new relationship.
Your society needs a bond of love
In order to develop and flourish.

Love is not merely God's holy wish—
It's His command for the good of man.
You can't exhaust love by loving—
It increases and spreads day by day.

Love has a rhyme and a reason
Of its own in this world of nature.
So, never be afraid of loving, as such,—
As the Lord shall bless you from above.

~

3. Who can manage a Burning Heart?

Lead your life as you should wish—
This is not the present-day mantra.
The management gurus would like to say—
'Manage life since it's a complex yantra.'*

We know life is not a simple thing;
It doesn't follow any beaten formulae.
Each life is different from the other—
You can't treat all the people equally.

Yet it's too difficult to manage a life—
This doesn't bloom like a pretty rose.
Life is full of thorns as we know—
And very tough as far as it goes.

Everything is manageable, the M—gurus say—
But who can manage a burning heart?
One can only manage the simple things—
Handling delicate things is quite an art.

---

* An apparatus or machine

4. Let Me Be a Host

Let me be a host, Oh Lord,
To all those who seek shelter.
Let me be a host, Oh Lord,
To all those who need daily bread.

Let me wrap them up, Oh Lord,
Who are shivering in cold.
Let me be a walking stick
To all who are feeble and old.

Let me feel their aches and pain
Who are shattered in their life.
Let me prop them up, Oh Lord,
Who are stooping under burden.

Let me sing a hymn to you, Lord,
For all those who lost their faith.
Let me spread your nice message
For all who wish to rise and walk.

5. Love is sharing

To your fiancée
Or to the dear wife,
Love is more than
Half the life.

Together we live
And together we die,
She is more than
What am I!

This is the true
Spirit of love;—
Togetherness is
The bond of love.

More than sharing
Your everyday foods,
Love is sharing
The vibgyor of moods.

More than your
Everyday reason—
Love is sharing
Life's true vision.

6. God has a Mission in You

A man is a man is a man
And that is all that you can
Have as the highest of births
In this wide physical world.

You're the king of all animals
And you're the ruler of this earth;
So, try to be as good as God
Who sends you for His mission.

Endeavour to be a Samaritan
And try to help those in need.
He's the best who helps of his own,
Without being asked for aid.

The Eastern Monk* once said—
'Where do you seek for God,
Except in front of your eyes?
There he exists in many forms.'

One who loves all His creatures,
Does serve the Lord indeed!

---

*   Swami Vivekananda

7. I am the One who can feel

When I am near the road,
I can hear the sound of speed.
When I am near the sea,
I can hear the waves break.

When I am near the forest,
I can hear the crickets chirp.
When I am near the lake,
I can hear the breeze pass by.

When I am in the home,
I can hear the wind groan.
When I am in the bed,
I can hear the bedbugs talk.

I am the one, who cannot see,
But who can feel the life around.
I am the one, who cannot run,
But who can crawl into eternity.

8. The Real Slum dog

Buildings daily rise, they are very tall.—
There are huge slums where people crawl.
Or, slums are bulldozed, huts daily fall—
City Improvement Boards care for all!

Slum-dwellers don't live but only survive.—
They get up at dawn, sharply at five,
And toil hard for bread in the city-hive.
They're poor and ill-paid, but very naïve.

They do all sorts of hazardous task,
But for right wages they hardly ask.
They're fated to toil from dawn to dusk,
Yet wear plain faces and no extra mask.

They sleep on footpath or in drain-pipe—
Their fruit of fortune is seldom ripe.
Slum dog millionaire is mere hype—
They belong to the 'obedient servant' type!

9. My Fate of a Eunuch

Please excuse me if I often fail;
Please excuse me if I set out to sail
To a distant island or a new cape
In order to get rid of life or escape.

Please excuse me if I don't help my brother;
Please excuse me if I don't save my mother
From the social dishonour she faces
Or, fail to stop daily feuds of friendly races.

Please excuse me if I slip from my duty;
Please excuse me if I ignore the beauty
Of this unique planet we are in
Where the entire mankind is my kin.

Please excuse me if I am not humane;
Please excuse me if I am no longer sane.
Here I feel myself a eunuch of a lonely man
Who waits for his exit in a ramshackle van.

10. I am a Little Pawn

Here I am a little helpless pawn,
Placed at the frontiers of battle.
I stand guard from dusk to dawn—
Even if my bones shiver and rattle.

I can't withdraw from the battle of life,
Nor can I make a retreat from my post.
A pawn has no friend or a dear wife—
Ere dying, he becomes a living ghost.

Always we move forward, do or die—
To save the elite from the opponent,
Who attack us even if we're too shy.
We ever stay in the field and not in tent.

The rook or knight, the queen or king—
All of them push us ahead to fight.
They're in the castle; we're in the ring—
Inferior chessmen, we have no right.

11. Be Content with what You Get

The sky has no limit, you know,
Yet the sky is the limit, they say.
Mark the sky where you'd go
Till your final jobbing day!

If you retire with sheer discontent
And don't climb to the top of the elm,
Would you feel yourself sad and bent
And unsuccessful at the helm?

Life is, some say, a journey by boat—
This is often not so smooth-sailing.
There are storms when it's hard to float,
Or times when you smile or be ailing.

The sky is there to beckon at you
When you try to reach its dome.
Assure that failure is nothing new—
So strive hard and be rooted at home.

12. I am a Walking Doll

At the behest of my own footfalls
I do only move forward—
Like the wound-up walking doll
That suddenly wants to stop
Whenever its breath fails him.

At every footstep of this life
I've ever walked along the road
On some mechanical inspiration,
Tottering now left and now right,
Alone, without a seeming balance.

So many hidden and nagging wishes
Have occasionally surfaced like a flash
At every turn of my dream avenue.

Now, on this rainy evening of life,
The ragged breathless doll alone
Crimps and limps on with salty drops
Rolling down all over his body,
And picks lost tears from the road.

13. The Global Identity

I am a man of this global city;
And I have no other identity.

If you write a simple essay on man,
Say all blood is red for every clan.

All eyes are eyes, black or blue—
Count the teeth till thirty two.

The world is now a big city,
People have many images
With only one identity.

Love them all with no pity;
Man is basically good,
With his divine heredity.

14. Light at the End of Darkness

There is light at the end of the tunnel,
However faded it might seem to be.
You are to wade through the darkness
Of the night and reach there finally.

There may be people waiting for you
And eager to know if you are alive;
For they think you might have been dead
Or, given up all your efforts to survive.

Born alone, you are to struggle alone!
Remember the world is a difficult place
And, God helps those who keep on trying.
So, do awake and run to finish the race.

Darkness isn't the end of everything,
However troubled you might have been.
In the light of darkness your mettle is seen;
So, turn it to be your new beginning!

15. Play Your Chess

The black squares and the white—
The black squares or then white,
You can't occupy more than a half—
None of you on your own behalf.

If you lose a pawn or other piece,
You are less than half of this!
Life's so critically arranged for you,
You can't have more or have it new.

Chess is the game of two warring forces—
Where you have no extra resources.
When you find you're losing the game,
Shouts will rise, 'shame, shame, shame!'

And if you somehow happen to win,
You'll gain all along with the queen.
Chess is not a mere game of chance—
The problem is you can play for once!

16. Love has to be Sincere

If you want to love, forget yourself—
Think of your beloved, come to her help.
Don't try to woo her at the first sight—
Meditate her face, that'll be right.

Don't be a Byron, but a Plato in love—
Leave everything to Cupid above.
When he'll shoot his timely arrow,
She'd become a loving sparrow.

Feeling of love is indeed exotic—
Love isn't pure physical or erotic.
Try to find the exact match you seek,
'Mind for mind' would be a nice pick.

Be sincere in love, and you'll win—
Your heart shall be pure and clean.
Love will bring you joy and pleasure—
Life will be full beyond any measure!

17. Snake-and-Ladder Game

There's no ceiling to your fortune—
No matter you ride it late or too soon.
You don't know at which turn luck waits—
The game of snake and ladder has baits.

You don't know at which turn it waits—
Climb up the ladder with nice gaits.
When you fall in the mouth of snake,
Accept it calmly for the game's sake!

Not always fortune favours the brave—
Heroes, too, often fight to their grave.
Fortune may also favour a chosen few,
With crowns of diamond, grand and new.

Ladder or snake—don't lose your heart,
Playing only matters, style is the art!
In the game of life, neither be glad or sad—
It is predestined, you know, good or bad.

18. A Coin has Two Sides

A coin has two sides, you know—
When you toss it, one doesn't show.
When you toss it on your thumbnail,
The coin falls flat, showing head or tail.

One side is up, and one is hidden,
Don't see the bottom, it's forbidden.
'Head I win' and 'tail you lose'—
This is not fair, if you are to choose.

You're to follow the rules of game—
If you happen to lose, it's not a shame.
If your side is not up and seen,
Your defeat is clear and clean.

When your luck is on your side,
Any horse may win that you ride.
And when you bet a losing horse,
It'll bring you to a good remorse!

19. Gateway of India

Phonegate or foodgate or coalgate—
Present India is surely marching on.
My India is now mature and great—
I can be proud of her as a crippled son.

The poor is poor, stuck in abject poverty;
They're but a 'minority of forty per cent'!
The rich has to grow richer in property—
So, 'ignore those who're naïve and innocent'!

Democracy is resilient and can remould itself.
So, pick out the weeds and cast them away—
This is the golden rule that comes to help.
The prize of harvest you'll reap some day.

Shine India, shine like a bright sun today;
The world's again waiting for your great show.
Discover the aureole of Bharat anyway—
And secure a global seat in the front row!

20. Life is a Golden Gift

Life is a golden gift—
So don't please abuse it.
Born in the shape of God,
You should never be slipshod.

Love is the nectar of life—
Love all and forget any strife.
Love is essential for you—
So let it widen your view.

Love ever makes you content
With life as a good present.
So let it blossom in full
And make it your golden rule.

Life has its ups and downs
As Fortune smiles or frowns.
Love is your real key to happiness
That heaven has bestowed to bless.

21. Happiness is a Precious Prism

People want to buy happiness at any cost;
It's our lifetime wish and principal goal.
And you have nothing if happiness is lost—
Everybody tries to get it heart and soul.

But you can't buy happiness with money,
Or you can't buy happiness at market.
It's the dearest and rarest commodity;
You can't just pick it up in your basket.

I think happiness is a precious prism
That reflects an illuminating glow—
Life becomes a charming experience
When we wish death be late and slow.

Still happiness is a mirage for most of us
That tantalizes man to the endgame.
For life's strewn with a mosaic of sorrows,
And I'm certain to lose with humid shame.

22. Resurrection of Pain

My pains repeatedly come around me—
I wonder why they speak so often!

Only their faces change from time to time,
Or else, they're the same as before, alas!

I've seen the images of many a pain
And kept them in a casket of my heart.

From childhood to adolescence,
And from adolescence to my youth—
My reporting on pain differs every time.

And, now the shadow of pain spreads
Over the western horizon today—
New and new pain eats into my soul.

I wonder as to whom I shall dedicate
My accumulated offerings of pain!—
I still carry on since the pains are there.

My pains are very dear and precious.
Let them all belong to me and enjoy
Themselves after each resurrection!

23. In the Time of Aching Twilight

I am in great pains, oh Friend,
I am obviously in great pains!
I shall, of course, no longer play
Hide and seek with friendly Death.

But I have a single request to him,
I have a single desire for him to fulfil—
Let him once bow in obeisance to me
And let my current birth be successful!

I've been a bit garrulous with him,
And so long I've deceived him much.
I have no fraudulent plans any more—
Let him lay the carpet of welcome!

I've been in great pains for long, oh Friend,
And I'm about to reach the twilight zone!
Time is now ripe for me to cheerfully
Step down from my egoist throne.

24. My Pains are Bubbles Now

I have had aches and pains—
They have long been with me.
My mind partly forgot about it—
Maybe they sank beneath senses.

Now they have been inspired again
To finally rise through gas as bubbles
And float on my mind's wavy surface.
My benign pains are calling me again!

25. Be Afraid of Danger
till it comes

Never be afraid of your sacred duties,
However difficult they might have been.
For the wise men have often warned—
Fear the ferocious until it's seen.

But as soon as the danger comes to you,
You should take all the right remedies.
A lion isn't a lion if you pull it by its mane—
Courage is mightier than fear or cowardice.

A thing that has to be collected,
A thing that has to be rightly given,
Or a task that has to be accomplished—
All should be done very fast and even.

There are men who make mistakes
And hence make their life miserable.
Almighty Time sucks your life-force
If you ignore duties on the timetable!

26. Let us finish the Job Tonight

Come; let us do some of the work today.
Who knows if we'll live or die tomorrow!
Let us finish the job tonight if we can—
And do it within the time left with us.

God knows what may happen in the morn—
Think the sun becomes a blue star, then!
Or, suppose I'll become a bird of smoke—
The mellow morning light will be in vain.

Hence I tell you to complete the job now—
Be it a win or loss, let's finish the game!

27. Homeless me

I've passed my time till sundown today
At various shelters scattered about—
In my rare moments of joy
Or, mostly, in the scare of life!

My bare appearance in the dewy dawn
Brightened in the scarlet rays of the sun.
I bathed in the sweet aura of late autumn.

In summer, monsoon, winter or spring,
I've changed my abode quite often.
Yet I remain homeless in this world.

At this sunset hill I now look back
And judge the jobs I've done in the day.—
The day's been spent in joys and sorrows
Since noonday heat till soft twilight.

I wonder why the burden of familiar
And unfamiliar days piles so heavy
In my tranquil nook of the evening!

28. Anger or Agony

Be it my anger or agony—
I do often feel and find
Man is in utter distress.
Everything is not O.K.
With the woeful mankind!

The affluent often waste food
For the sake of sport or obesity.
But the unfed ones scramble
For it in the dustbins of the city.

Man is denied, oh! It's a pity,
His sacred right to live.—
But who knows why he is still
Denied his last right to die
In his peace and dignity?

29. Monotony

Our life here is monotony,
Sure, like a mirror that reflects
The same image every time,
And that's akin to an agony!

Our life is painted too dull
On the roughened canvas
With a plain brush of neglect—
Like two bones and a skull.

Man is an icon of many pains,
Finely sculpted by his family,
His friends and the followers
As well as the cipher citizens!

In the battle of life, death wins
As monotonously as ever—
Man painfully loses at last
The bout of virtues and sins!

30. The lost man in a Caravan

Man is often deserted,
As in a lost caravan
And plods on towards his doom
As miserably as he can!

The caravan belongs to him
And he belongs to the caravan—
Till the end they travel together
As cosily as they both can!

The caravan is his family
And the caravan is his fort;
They sail across life's history
Touching each human port.

Life is an endless desert
For many a wretched man—
He began to cross it with hopes,
But finally succumbs in the caravan!

31. Civility is dying

Man is an animal, free to think.
But he himself is seldom freed
From his ever-growing greed.
His self-content is sure to sink!

Men rush for honour and wealth
In quite an endless rat race.
But they can't keep the pace
And slip into dire ill-health!

Man only weighs his loss or gain—
He has no scope to be sentimental
Or to believe in the transcendental.
Life never gives you relief from pain!

Man's no longer in good humour
And his distant vision is lost.
His aim is to gain at any cost—
Civility's now a bad tumour!

32. Missing Humanity

I don't know much of the nitty-gritty—
Man must have the basic humanity.
What's a man if he is not human—?
The beast is beast, and man is man!

You can't teach one to be humane
With either a carrot or a long cane.
Humanity oozes from the heart of man—
Like a stream that flows subterranean!

It's a feeling that kindles your heart
And prompts you to be a man apart.
You can feel the light in your soul—
By God's grace, you change your role!

Humanity's now vanished into the blue—
And the naïve people have hardly a clue.
Only one who has some grains of pity
Can think of ever attaining humanity!

33. Man is nomadic

Every man is nomadic in blood
And static only by civilization.
It's since Noah's times of flood
That man's the lord of migration.

Man travels from land to land,
From one continent to another.
He often leaves his own homeland
To visit his world-wide brother.

Man is a wanderer by nature,
And may have no bond with home.—
So he makes of him a global stature
By visits from Baghdad to Rome!

The wanderlust bug bites man through ages
As he sails by boat or in the winged ship.
He's been fond of breaking home-like cages
And tour the big globe on his perpetual trip.

34. In Search of Leisure

I won't be any more in bondage;
I won't be any more in enticement.
I'll leave the happy nook of my home,
And give up the warmth of my nest—
To set my wings in the distant skies
For a cool dip in the open light there.

I'll be no more perched in a golden cage—
Or, no more be locked in the rib-cage.
I'll put off my householder's robe,
And put off my adorned plumage—
To rig the sails in the soaring winds
For a long healing breath in free air.

If I go missing in search of my leisure,
Nobody may please misunderstand me!

35. Poetry is my old Confidante

Poetry is my old confidante—
I can confide my secrets in her.
In the storms and tempests of life
I only follow her wish and advice.

I do not love my wife so much
As I very often do love her.
I can leave my home or the world
On a single request from her!

All over her soft body of words
I sketch my love day and night.
If she turns away for a moment,
I lose all my cherished hopes.

At the rhythm of her light feet
All my infatuation is redeemed.
Poetry is my beautiful confidante—
All my revolts are on her behalf!

36. Raise your Fist, oh Brother!

Raise your fist, oh brother, raise your fist!
Hold your head high and up in the air—
Your chosen rulers have been corrupted,
Let them repent and leave the chair!

'Down with tyrants', 'Down with betrayers'—
Raise your slogan with a lion's voice.
They'll be shaken to the core of their heart
And forced to opt for the ousting choice.

You're free to choose your government
In a democracy, run by the tax you pay.
You have the right to dislodge it sometimes
And elect another and able one any day!

Change your ruler as often as you need—
People are the real kingmakers today.
Vote for the best representatives you find
And make them answer for all they do or say!

37. Animals are Luckier

Man shouldn't ever be called free
Until all his brethren are unchained.
No man should sleep, fasting a night—
God's beloved, he be not disdained!

Earth is the abode for various animals—
That's true for all, except the king of them.
Man makes homes for the pets he keeps—
In his own case, it's a different game.

The farmer grows food for the others,
Yet he remains unfed or emaciated.
It's a riddle that often puzzles me—
Why from the rest is he dissociated?

He grows food by the sweat of his brow—
Still he's often denied his own food.
Animals are lucky to have their providence—
But men fast to die as they never should!

38. Humanity is yet to Develop

I've been in the dense jungle of life and
Seen the intense struggle for survival.
Man is sometimes less than a beast and
Labeled as the shame of an animal.

I've seen him eat wild roots and boiled leaves;
I've seen him eat raw palm fruit for days;
I've seen him make salt out of a puddle
And dwell in a sty where the pig lives!

Man is not yet the lord of animals—
Humanity is yet to develop a lot.
Animals still find their food and shelter—
It's a pity that human beings cannot!

Man is too greedy to share anything
Which is a common gift of nature.
Men need not be noble but equal—
Since all are born the same in stature!

39. My Bond with Roots

I had once a relationship with wife,
But I had no bond
That binds us together for life!

I had once a relationship with the flower,
But I had no bond
That links me with it anywhere!

I had once a relationship with the Pole Star,
But I had no bond
That illuminates me from afar!

I had once a relationship with sunshine,
But I had no bond
That brings me the warmth of wine!

I had once a relationship with my society,
But I had no bond
That fastens two souls with love or pity!

I had once a relationship with my roots,
And I have still a bond
That enlivens me with everyday shoots!

40. A Platonic Love-story

I don't wish to see your present mirror image,
Oh, my dream-girl of the college life!
You were then hardly seventeen or so,
And I was an undergraduate of English.

You were my divine lady of those days,
And I was a poor Platonic lover.
I didn't want to disturb you by revealing
My hidden-in-the-heart love for you.

Only the thing I wanted was to see you,
Once in a blue moon on my way to market.
Sometimes I took a short round-about
So that I could have a sudden look at you.

But just in a year you were married away
To a gentleman who shook me to the core.
You have that eighteen-year image stuck
On my retina that I won't disturb anymore!

41. The Game of Politics

Politics is the game of fine idiots
Where democracy is on the gallows.
It's a feast for manoeuvring leaders
And a bitter pill the citizen swallows!

There are very few good statesmen
Who put their land above their lust.
Leaders want to pauperize the poor
And ignore the ignorant like dust!

Money and muscle still elect many of them
Who aim to amass ill-gotten wealth.
When government is formed by horse-trading,
Could you wish democracy a good health?

The continued greed of the pet leaders
And their petty ego of superiority
Have tied the masses to their dismal fate.—
It's time for a revamp and fresh priority.

42. The World is full of Half-wits

The learned can't plain speak an inch—
It's their classical problem!
The illiterate can't embellish their speech—
So we may excuse them!

But the real fun is with half-pundits—
They can pop words like yellow corns.
Those go astray and bring no plaudits—
They should be decked as unicorns.

The world is full of half-wits like me—
They're between the fool and the wise.
We know little but profess much, you see,
Like a Jack of all trades we rise!

But half is ever half, like a semi-circle—
It doesn't grow to be full.
As half-cut diamonds seldom sparkle
And are discarded as a rule!

43. Live to Love and love to live

When you really feel 'I am yours,
And you are only mine',
Know it then for sure—
It's the day of valentine!

If you feel your heart opens
To someone you think dear,
Know then love happens—
It's so deep and clear!

The V-day doesn't come
Once a year as you think.
It happens as often as some
Feelings in you turn pink.

When you think the unknown
Person is so familiar to you,
Over the ages you've known—
Be sure love is nothing new.

So live to love and love to live.
This is the rule He sets above.
For God wants you all to give
Your most precious gift of love!

44. It's my Dear Destiny

When I talk with myself
In front of the mirror,
Then appears my inner self
With a look of horror.

Sometimes it grins at me
With a crooked smile,
Or, it chides or warns me,
Or fumes with bitter bile!

My dual self shakes me to the root,
And gives me a cold shiver—
I'm left hanging down on a foot,
Ready to plunge into Mortal River!

I am afraid of the looks I can see,
As the looking glass reflects my image—
I think it is my dear destiny
That lies in wait in every Age.

Whenever I talk to myself alone
In a corner of the solitary cell,
The image asks me to atone
For the sins and wrongs I can't tell!

45. Everyman without a Soul

Once I read while solving a crypto quip
That three things must a man should
Have, if his soul would live, (says the quip)—
These are bread, beauty and brotherhood!

That poet was a seer and an idealist—
Nobody would now live for his soul.
In today's rat race every man is a finalist
Who aims to have the body as a whole!

Still I feel the poet was quite right—
Man is not a beast but the best animal.
He has a mind and a deep insight—
Still, oh! He's not kind to a decimal!

Those who aim the soul, miss the mark.—
Man has no time to stare at beauty;
Brotherhood for him is also dark.—
He only frets with his bread-earning duty!

46. I am a Democratic Idiot

I am no doubt a democratic idiot
And an everyman out of his humour.
If not malignant, life is sure a tumour—
Death is welcome as an angel's chariot!

The soul, we know, soars through heaven
To reach its original divine destination.
The goal of man is more than seven*—
Death is humane when man lives by ration.

I have been a fool all through my life.—
Nobody could alter my earned belief.
It was so fast and it was so deep—
Seldom had I got love from all or wife!

Democracy is an idiot's refuge, like mine.
It's also the shelter for a habitual rogue.
Still it's the modern man's only vogue—
The lifeline people cherish like red wine!

47. Believe as long as you live

If man seeks happiness, he gets sorrow—
It's true of today, as of tomorrow.
When he seeks pleasure, he gets pain—
Instead of love, he has disdain.

The peace of mind is an illusion—
It's filled with stress and delusion.
All around us there's war and death;
There's a big distrust and lack of faith.

Man was born free in the by-gone age
And he rose to be a saint or a sage.
Today he has misery all around—
His wants and woes now abound.

He has little joy or no big hope—
For him, life's a walk on tight rope.
All isn't bleak though, he still believes—
For man believes as long as he lives!

48. Let us Revolt Now

Snap my chains with your axe
And let me be as free as born.
I had no wish on my birthday
To be thus chained and torn!

Chained to the peg ever since,
A beast of burden, too, has scorn.
Although not fated to fetters,
Some toil to die since the morn.

My legs are chained, ah! poor as I am!
Yet I have a pair of free horns.
Remember the poor will get a chance
To butt you down and break the corns!

The path is not rosy, we know,
And maybe it's laid with thorn.
Still it's inspiring for all those slaves
Who are denied the right to corn.

Let's now revolt, oh all the 'brutes'!
We have nothing to lose but scorn.
We must, no doubt, be invincible—
For, we're blessed since when born!

49. Let me sing Once more

Please return my song
To my lips
And let me sing it once more—
I'll do a hymn in her praise
And sing the forgotten lore.

Please return my walk
To my legs
And let me stroll along the shore—
The breeze is there to welcome
And thrill me to the core.

Please return my flight
To my wings
And let me fly in the open sky—
As happy as the white clouds,
I'll float up above so high!

Please return the noise
To my ears
And let me hear the sullen cry—
I'll try to soothe her sorrow
And heal the wounds dry.

50. Your victory is in sight

When your sky is cloudy,
It may often rain;
When your sky is cloudy,
The sun may hide, again.

When your sky is sunny,
The world appears golden.
When your sky is sunny,
Your horizons embolden.

When your day's a dark night,
You like to hide your face.
When your day's very bright,
You're sure to win the race.

Man makes a day or night,
As he wishes to win or lose.
Man creates the gloom or light—
Head or tail you're to choose.

Night ends in daybreak
And the day travels to night;
If you can do the whole trek,
Your victory is sure in sight.

51. I feel Checkmated

The wise men often say, 'What is fated,
There's little chance it can be abated!'
I'm an example of one so ill-fated—
The wise, in my case, are proven true.

I rose quite slow and belated.
My nemesis seems to be instigated
To make me a loser and checkmated!—
My life-tree seldom hopefully grew.

My achievement has been so truncated
That beyond all measure I feel hated.
Today I think I'm quite outdated—
That's a right conclusion I ever drew.

While nature's beauty is so variegated,
It pains me, my joys were aerated
And my thirst was never satiated—
My wine of life ever failed to brew!

My rightful ambitions were thwarted
While agonies or sorrows rarely abated.
The result is I've been utterly frustrated—
My Nemesis is sure a cold-blooded shrew.

52. Beauty comes from within

Once upon a time I met my dream-girl,
My sweetheart, in a short day dream—
She was just then using an ordinary
Not-so-nice and cheap beauty cream.

"Is your public beauty so cheap",
I asked the tall celebrity dame,
"Or, is it a justice, oh my darling,
To your renowned aesthetic fame?"

Hearing my harsh words, she gave
Her million-dollar signature smile,
With a heart-rending killer flash
That seemed an attempt to beguile!

Yet I repeated my next question
Humbly in a submissive voice,
"What's the secret of your beauty
Oh lady, and what's the wise choice?"

It was her silent but eloquent reply
That obviously means to say,
"Beauty comes from within, oh dear,
And, look, it shines like a spring day."

53. To my Heavenly Love

Your age doesn't exceed sixteen,
Though I'm crossing sixty one.
The earth's turned many a round
But you're static since I've seen.

Age can't wither your image away
From the arena of my eye-ball.
Oh, my youngest goddess in heaven,
I don't want you to ever fall!

Your idol is set on my frame of heart
Since when I've been a boyish student.
You're still my Muse, as sweet as ever—
Maybe I'm now old and a bit prudent.

You're my heavenly love, oh you fairy!
I wish you should ever remain so.
I don't want anybody to dethrone you—
Stay with me in every world that I go!

54. The Sonnet about a Shirt

This blue-and-white striped shirt
Suits me nicely in these days—
This is what my loyal friends would say.

The world doesn't move on buttery words.
So many times I've requested them—
'Please don't leg-pull me for fun's sake!

'Don't collect collyrium from clouds
And smear my eye lines with it—
Let me be myself as ugly as I look'.

I know only the character counts,
No matter what you wear or put on—
Every shirt, black or pink, suits you!
Nothing suits me a bit now, I know—
But nobody tells me the plain truth, ah!

55. Hostile Brotherhood

Oh my Sanaullah! Oh dear Sarabjit!
You've never seen or faced each other—
Still you're enemies since independence.
You have nothing in common, oh brother!

Each of you were a criminal before law
In the alien land where you were jailed
And where you were killed by violence
And where humanity miserably failed.

You could have been friends but for the border—
You could have been brothers but for hatred!
It's the partition that made you enemies—
A relation that could have been sacred!

Alas! Day by day the line grows thick
And freedom still crawls on all the fours.
Ill-will is a skewed vision you won't see.—
Oh, martyrs of hate! don't close your doors!

56. Bina Kalindi and her team

Bina Kalindi is no more a mere name,
No more so is Sangita Barui or Afsana Khatun—
They made us proud and brought us shame,
As did the burnt child Roushenara Khatun!

They have a common offence and shared sin—
It's their right to live as nicely as they want.
Hence they rose up against their dear kin.
In their battle of life as the laws do grant!

All of them protested against child marriage—
All they craved for was basic education.
And what they possess is sheer courage—
They're young but full of determination.

Bina and her team revolted against their families;
Nay, they rose up against their own dark fate.
Bravo! Girls, you plan your own bold stories
And build your society with a fresh mandate!

57. Age of Marketing

This is the great age of marketing—
You can buy anything and everything,
From pure darkness to blue sunshine;
Buy it physically or you buy online!

You're only to place the exact order
For anything you like across any border.
The surreal virtues will be tailor-made,
And the indelible vices will never fade.

The USP is really an obsessive hype
For any upcoming product of any type.
You can buy a good wife or a whore—
You can buy envy or spite or more.

But you can't purchase the thing you need—
Since none can buy character-growing seed.
You can't buy any love or faith or humanity—
No agency can market such a commodity!

58. Still I want to live

I want to live, oh brother,
I want to live!
Please give me a lease of new life,
Please do give!

The world is so cruel that it won't
Let me survive—
When I felt I was dying,
I had a fresh drive!

But it was too late, oh brother,
Death's now seized me!
My ailment is so terminal that there's
No escape from destiny!

Still I want to live, oh brother,
Want to live more!
But my time's up over here
On life's sea-shore!

59. My Journey is over

Time's running out, Friend,
My time is running out!
Please hold my rudder, Captain,
I'll son be leaving aside!

The ship has crossed the channel
Through the long days of storm—
Now there'll be calm waters ahead
On my journey as a norm!

The boat's touched many a port
On its scheduled trip to lands.
Many people came to associate
And made various demands.

Now twilight casts its last glow
Over my vast western horizon—
I'm ready to land at the last point
And have a long rest till the pain's gone!

60. Never be biased

When the sun goes dark, or the
Moon becomes too bright,
Most people would say
Everything is not right!

But there are certain times
When such things may happen.
So keep your head straight
And the mind clear and open.

There's nothing, they say,
Absolutely right or wrong.
People subjectively judge
Every book, dish or song!

Dark clouds may hide the sun
Or, the full moon shine as day;
Man should never be biased
To weigh a thing either way!

61. It's easy to give Sermons

It's so easy to give sermons, oh dear,
But very difficult to follow them!
You may list tens of commandments,
Yet abide by a few, to your shame!

Be it an ethical or social lesson
Or a piece of friendly advice—
Some people are wont to ignore it
Or, seldom consider it as nice!

People like religious monks
May take it to their heart and
Carry out the sermons in full,
To make their living a nice art.

It's the faith and strength in you
That prompts you to follow them.
You can earn an awe of the masses
Who'll make a niche for your fame!

62. Divinity is the Goal

Man shall die, today or tomorrow—
And I'm not shocked at this truth.
Life on earth begins or ends
With a note of pain or sorrow.

In between, he has pleasures or joy
Which we call dear happiness!
But man's so blind about his fate
That he acts like a robotic toy.

Yet his goal is sure divinity—
As he's the cream of creation.
Man should ever try to be a god,
Even if he needs an infinity!

Man should overcome the fear of death
In his eternal quest for light.
Remember death's also a part of life
In your spiritual scheme of faith.

63. You are my Guardian

Forgive me, oh my God of life,
Forgive me for my incompetence!
I've failed to lead my life as you wish,
Owing to my conceit and pretence.

Arrogance has kept me away from you
And shrouded my vision as well.
I didn't feel you were watching me
Ever in whatever I did act or tell!

You are my guardian, oh Lord of life,
You are my innermost soul.
Blindly I roam about in the jungle
And ignore your parental role!

Excuse me, oh Master, in this birth
And let me learn your loving lesson,
So that I don't go astray any more
And make my life meaningful as a son!

64. Human life is a golden Gift

One life isn't enough, oh my friend,
To enjoy the beauties of this earth.
My desires are not fulfilled as yet,
And I require more than one birth.

Everybody knows there's no end
To the charms of this pretty world.
But our transient life is too short—
That none seems to have quarrelled.

So make sure you don't waste time,
Since you may not get another life.
Human life is a nice golden gift,
Since man is a creature of unique type.

Make the best use of life you've got
During the limited span you're here.
Enjoy the pied beauty of nature,
For, you may not be reborn, oh dear!

65. You are my Companion

You've given me every right, oh master!
You've given me every freedom
To shape my own life as I wish
In the given sphere of my kingdom!

You're my father, you're my lord,
You are indeed my best friend.
You're my sole confidant in distress
You're my companion to the end.

I've not been aware of the evil—
Please do protect me from it.
It often lurks from behind me
And pushes me down in the pit.

You're the best judge, oh my lord.—
I believe you guide me from within.
I'll abide by what you wish and tell—
Please save me from every vice or sin!

66. Master has a different Design

Brick by brick the design is laid
As bricks build up an edifice.
And moments pile upon moments,
When moments build up my life.

Bricks are die-cast and are the same—
They add to quite a regular shape.
But the blocks of life aren't uniform—
So they defy all the known designs.

My life's been a jumble of moments—
A total disarray of joy and sorrows.
I couldn't tidy up my only one life
And have what is called the peace!

I think the Master has a different design
And He gave me less than I deserve.
Maybe he'd compensate the next time—
So I have to be patient and honour him!

67. Man is not human

God's true descendent is man—
But alas! He's been bitten by Satan!
So he often goes the satanic way
And fears not the dark, but the day!

It's painful that man becomes a beast—
He rapes or kills, not ashamed to the least!
Man is so cruel that beasts take a beat—
In animal world, he has a back seat!

He has no need, but is fond of crime—
He cares for no necessity or the time.
Beasts are beasts and man is man,
Yet beasts can't be so vile, as he can!

It's a pity man is no more human—
It's also sad that he's an heir to Satan.
Man should emulate his Lord above
And win over all with care and love.

68. This Moment is Eternal

Dewdrops sparkle like diamonds
On the grass tops in the autumn morn,
And the sunshine invites me to its joy
When I'm ready to bathe in delight.

The sky is clear and wears a pure blue
And the chilly wind is rather welcome.
The flowers in the garden greet me gladly
Along with all the floating butterflies.

Everything around seems to be idyllic
As if I am in a nice dreamland alone.
Blessed and happy in the nature's lap,
I wish this moment should be eternal!

Man once lived in the happiness of Eden
But he's no more as lucky since his exile.
Still he gets a few lost glimpses of joy
When his mind is clean and transparent.

69. I am a Masked Man

I am a masked man, oh, a masked man!
And I can't reveal my true self to others!
I put on a hard shell to hide my softness,
Or say, my weakness to my brothers!

I have a hidden ego which pricks me,
Which prods me to act against wish.
It often prompts me to behave wrongly
Like a man who is mad and selfish!

I am a social captive who abides by
A lot of bad laws and is forbidden
To act according to his conscience.
So he feels scared and stays hidden.

Even the rulers aren't citizen-friendly;
So I cannot protest against the evil.
I'm not alone in the team of cowards—
I am a masked man, and not a devil!

70. Innocence is pure Joy

I wish to be as innocent as a child
That I had been till my boyhood.
But innocence is now too soon lost
And children grow fast to adulthood.

Innocence is pure and natural joy—
An uninterrupted flow of divinity.
In the whirlpool of pace and greed
Man has lost his valued integrity.

In the cyber age of advancement
Little is kept back under the child lock—
Children don't have to struggle hard
To reach the zone once forbidden.

Innocence is a precious gift to the child
Which very often we let him violate.
The loss of innocence brings misery
And makes him prone to crime and hate.

71. Polish counts more than Purity

I am now much worn and torn
Like a nine-year-old ragged shirt
Which can no longer protect me
From the social heat, cold or dirt!

When I looked grand in my new dress,
People watched and obeyed me with awe.
Now that I'm in a torn image before them,
They view me like a rain-soaked jackdaw.

My shirt isn't any more honoured,
Nor its wearer regarded with respect.
This is the way of the world, they say—
Nothing better you should expect.

Old is not gold, as people would believe.
But when the gold is old, it looks pale.
Polish now counts more than purity—
Shirts are fine, though men aren't hale!

72. Man becomes a Saint

The true man isn't a local man,
He lives and dwells beyond it.
Animals live in a lair or den,
But humans have no such limit.

Every great man is a world man—
He doesn't live for his community.
Ever he transcends selfish goals
And strives to enrich humanity.

His religion doesn't bind him to
Any parochial ideas or narrow creed.
He believes in the religion of man
And lives for ideals beyond all greed.

Man becomes a saint in this life by
His concern for mankind as a whole.
Seldom have they died after death
Who are remembered for their role.

73. A Dead man's Song

I'm now dead; I know how it feels to be alive.
The world around here doesn't allow
Me to live the chosen way I want to.

I remember I fought since when I was five
And felt myself an alien who has to bow
Before his own people in his slit land to

Get an animal's life as a gift and survive,
In exchange of dirty child labour, now
Banned in the civilized society all through.

I was put up to rear as if in a big bee-hive
Of tents for homeless refugees, and saw how
A weekly petty cash dole that they drew

From the kind government kept us alive!
All the while I lived I hated death,
All the while I lived I abhorred life.

For, only a living man asks, 'what is death?'
Or, only a dying man asks, 'what is life?'
Yet I'm now dead and don't want to be alive!

74. Death is their Panacea

Death is the panacea, they say, for the poor
From the famished sub-Saharan Africa
To the arid lands of Indian sub-continent.

It is the cure-all of every evil and pain,
Perpetrated to them by their fellow men
In their cruel lust for power and wealth.

But this was surely not a thing to happen;
For, men are born to live, and not to die!

Ignorance is the anaesthesia of the poor
And the downtrodden all over the world.
Liberate them so that they should revolt
And earn their bread, shelter and health.
They should denounce death till they live
And secure a niche in the history of man!

So let the poor rise together and herald
The advent of a bold New Age once again!

75. Reborn in Bengal

Let me quietly die today
And be reborn tomorrow
In a remote village of Bengal
With the freedom of fishermen;
Or, as a blacksmith or a potter
As they used to be, say, long
Four or five hundred years ago.

You might give me a name
To call, like Jadu, Hari or Ramen
As I'd live with my little daughter.
I'd spread my net to catch fish
From my slim-bodied canoe
Into the shallow slender stream
That pours into the river Ganga.

Or, think, I would leisurely finish
Making my daily pots on the wheel
With no hurry, as if in a day-dream;
Or, maybe my family job changes
To shape up iron tools on my anvil,
With the liberty of a lazy kingfisher.

So let me peacefully die today
Until I'm born as a village-fisher.

76. Find the Difference

People spend hugely on aromatherapy,
People spend so much on spa;
But there are more people here
Who can't have the aroma of boiled rice!

People often travel by jet planes,
People travel in luxury cruisers;
But there are more of my countrymen
Who can't afford to travel other than
By their bullock carts or pair of feet!

People wear leather jackets,
People wear pashmina or fur;
But there are millions of them here
Who keep themselves warm by the sun
Or the odd fire under the open sky!

Now find six differences, as they ask—
That's your only next-Gen home task!

77. Between Life and Death

They don't remember me any more—
They're my friends who live ashore.
I'm now tossing on the hostile waves,
I'm now tossing on the angry waves.

They're quiet in their abode of peace
While I'm exiled in the far cruel seas.
I don't have any island in view—
Since I left and bade them adieu!

They understand me not any more—
But they aren't my enemies next door.
Yet I am, alas, forsaken and forlorn!
Between life and death, I'm still torn!

My friends are friends, and foes are foes
Since I passing through joys and woes.
They were with me on my life's trip—
I thank them all ere I go to sleep!

78. Man is a living Museum

My life is an ancient museum—
Since the age of Neanderthal man.
Perhaps I lived in the Altamira
And drew cave paintings with élan.

I live as eternal mummy of time
In an onyx coffin of Mayan Age.
I seldom grow here old or young
And believe in the ancient adage.

I've walked through the aeons,
I've dreamt through the aeons
In my quest for human perfection
Up the ladder steps of civilization.

I'm still laid in the closed coffin—
This remains as an old death-bin.
Man's a living museum of history—
In him lies the true creative mystery!

79. My Maladies defy Prognosis

My maladies grow in seclusion—
Those are of an esoteric kind.
I am always fond of an exotic pain
That brings tranquillity to mind.

I live to be benumbed to the core
And stay in a perpetual coma—
My pain require a strong sedative
To lead me to a full stop, not a comma.

Individual maladies have select remedies
Which the specialist can only prescribe.
But my maladies defy any prognosis
And are quite difficult to describe.

They're rather immune from therapeutics,
Hence I always have to suffer from them—
My maladies are unique and Age-centric;
So I have no escape from most of them!

80. You live when you feel Pain

I've often tried best to discover
The genesis of my continual pain.
And so I've visited many doctors—
But all my efforts went in vain!

I have a throbbing pain all the while I live.
Along with my pulse, it reminds me that
When you feel pain, be sure you live;
Because only the dead are quite happy!

You know the dead are beyond all pains;
And so happiness belongs to them—
You can't be happy and alive together,
Since my times are so inane to shame!

My efforts to find out the source of pain
Have never been fruitful, you know!
Life's a painful experience since birth
For those who put up a flopped show.